Landbird Monitoring in the Arctic Network

Gates of the Arctic National Park and Preserve and Noatak National Preserve (2010 Report)

Natural Resource Data Series NPS/ARCN/NRDS—2012/315

Kristin DeGroot and Jennifer McMillan

National Park Service
Arctic Network Inventory and Monitoring Program
4175 Geist Road
Fairbanks, AK 99709

April 2012

U.S. Department of the Interior
National Park Service
Natural Resource Stewardship and Science
Fort Collins, Colorado

The National Park Service, Natural Resource Stewardship and Science office in Fort Collins, Colorado, publishes a range of reports that address natural resource topics of interest and applicability to a broad audience in the National Park Service and others in natural resource management, including scientists, conservation and environmental constituencies, and the public.

The Natural Resource Data Series is intended for the timely release of basic data sets and data summaries. Care has been taken to assure accuracy of raw data values, but a thorough analysis and interpretation of the data has not been completed. Consequently, the initial analyses of data in this report are provisional and subject to change.

All manuscripts in the series receive the appropriate level of peer review to ensure that the information is scientifically credible, technically accurate, appropriately written for the intended audience, and designed and published in a professional manner.

This report received informal peer review by subject-matter experts who were not directly involved in the collection, analysis, or reporting of the data.

Views, statements, findings, conclusions, recommendations, and data in this report do not necessarily reflect views and policies of the National Park Service, U.S. Department of the Interior. Mention of trade names or commercial products does not constitute endorsement or recommendation for use by the U.S. Government.

This report is available from the Arctic Network Inventory and Monitoring Program (http://science.nature.nps.gov/im/units/arcn/index.cfm) and the Natural Resource Publications Management website (http://www.nature.nps.gov/publications/nrpm/).

Please cite this publication as:

NPS 185/113957, 189/113957, April 2012

Contents

Figures

Tables

Acknowledgments

The 2010 field season could not have been completed without input and hard work from a number of people. Thanks to J. Barnes and J. Schmidt for assistance with study design and planning. We'd like to thank NPS field staff H. Kristenson, S. Backensto and T. Pendergrast. Thank you also to our skilled volunteer, Jeff Walters. NPS pilot S. McMillan assisted with flights. Thanks to T. Whitesell and A. Rath for assisting with field gear organization and transportation of crews. The kind staff at Brooks Range Aviation flew us safely in and out of the field. A big thanks to D. Gardner, Z. Richter, N. Vasquez and the seasonal rangers at the Bettles Ranger Station for being our point-of-contact in the field and making sure we were safe. N. Bywater developed the database for this project.

Introduction

The Arctic Network Inventory and Monitoring program (ARCN) encompasses five park units including Gates of the Arctic National Park and Preserve (GAAR) and Noatak National Preserve (NOAT). The landbirds assemblage (passerines, near-passerines, raptors and galliformes) was chosen by the ARCN for long-term monitoring because it includes many species that spend the majority of their lives in terrestrial environments. Passerine birds comprise more than 50% of the bird species in ARCN. All ARCN park units are mandated under the Alaska National Interest Lands Conservation Act (ANILCA) to protect habitat for and various assemblages of avian species (U. S. Congress 1980). Under ANILCA [Section 201(8)], protection of populations of and habitat for waterfowl, raptors and other species of birds is specifically mandated in NOAT. In GAAR, the NPS is directed to protect habitat for and populations of raptorial birds. In addition, several international treaties, federal laws and initiatives provide protections for migratory birds and require action by NPS (Migratory Bird Treaty Act, Endangered Species Act, and North American Bird Conservation Initiative).

Landbirds were selected by ARCN as a vital sign because they are easily detected and are well studied across North America. Standardized methods for monitoring landbirds are well established and currently utilized by several networks across the country. Landbirds are an important component of park ecosystems, and their high body temperature, rapid metabolism, and high ecological position in most food webs make them good indicators of the effects of local and regional changes in ecosystems (Fancy and Sauer 2000). Changes in landbird ecology and demography have been demonstrated to be useful as indicators of global climate change (Sillett et al. 2000).

Specific objectives of the ARCN landbird monitoring program are to: 1) determine annual long-term trends in density and frequency of occurrence of 5-10 of the most commonly detected landbird species along selected river corridors across ARCN during the breeding season (June); 2) determine annual long-term trends in landbird species composition and distribution in selected sites across ARCN during the breeding season (June); and 3) improve understanding of breeding bird-habitat relationships and the effects of invasive plants and climatic changes on bird populations. These objectives will be met by correlating the population density of 5-10 of the most commonly detected landbird species with habitat composition and availability. Future changes in the population density of these species may correlate with changes in specific habitat variables.

The general sampling procedures for conducting these surveys will follow those established for the National Breeding Bird Survey (BBS) (Sauer et al. 2008), a roadside survey that we have adapted for river corridors in ARCN. Landbird surveys conducted by ARCN in June of 2010 will serve to supplement protocol development, staff training and refinement of methods. Survey methodology utilized by the BBS, Alaska Landbird Monitoring survey (ALMS), Guldager (2004) and Mitchell et al. (2009) will be adopted and refined by ARCN and continued annually for the long-term monitoring program.

Landbird monitoring methods for the long term must be established that 1) recognize potential limitations of the NPS wilderness minimum requirement standards in GAAR, 2) focus on common species, 3) are fungible, 4) are affordable, and 5) are reliable in producing the targeted metrics. Landbird surveys were conducted by ARCN in June of 2010 along the Noatak River from GAAR into NOAT and used repeat surveys by three separate crews to generate landbird population estimates The ARCN is collaborating with the Central Alaska Network so that landbird monitoring methods are comparable and based on occupancy methods in both networks.

In June, 2010 two park units (GAAR and NOAT) were surveyed by four skilled NPS staff and volunteers. The primary objectives of the 2010 survey effort were:

- Establish survey points and complete one river corridor survey that will be used for long-term monitoring efforts

- Test survey methodology to determine the feasibility of conducting repeated surveys using multiple crews along the same stretch of river for long-term landbird monitoring

Methods

Study Area

The Arctic Network includes five park units encompassing approximately 78,000 km^2 of mostly-roadless area (Figure 1). The area is dominated by the Brooks Range Mountains that run east to west through the park units. Elevation ranges from sea level to 2,553m. Vegetative cover in the lower slopes and riparian communities of the parks, where this study was conducted, consists mostly of tussock tundra and shrub thickets (Viereck et al. 1992).

This study was conducted on the Noatak River in GAAR and NOAT. This river was selected as a long-term monitoring site because it flows through two continguous park units and represents an east-west gradient through tundra-dominated habitat. Also, the Noatak River is relatively calm and, therefore, less-challenging to float, is accessible at many sites along its length and has been surveyed previously for landbirds (Guldager 2004).

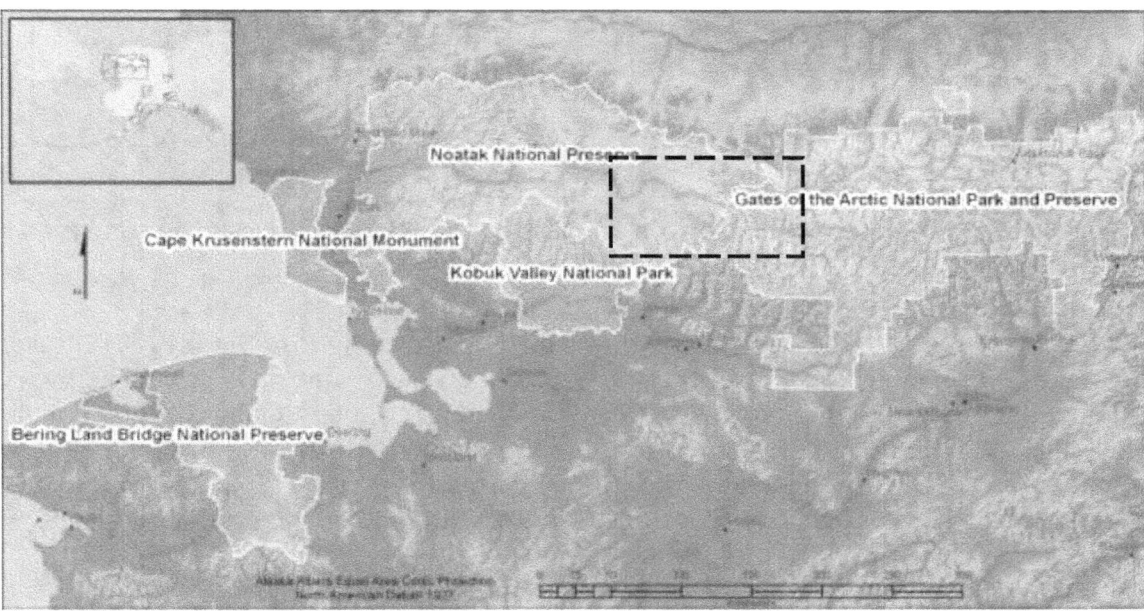

Figure 1. National Park units in the Arctic Network, Alaska. Bird surveys were conducted along the Noatak River in Gates of the Arctic National Park and Preserve and Noatak National Preserve indicated by the dashed box.

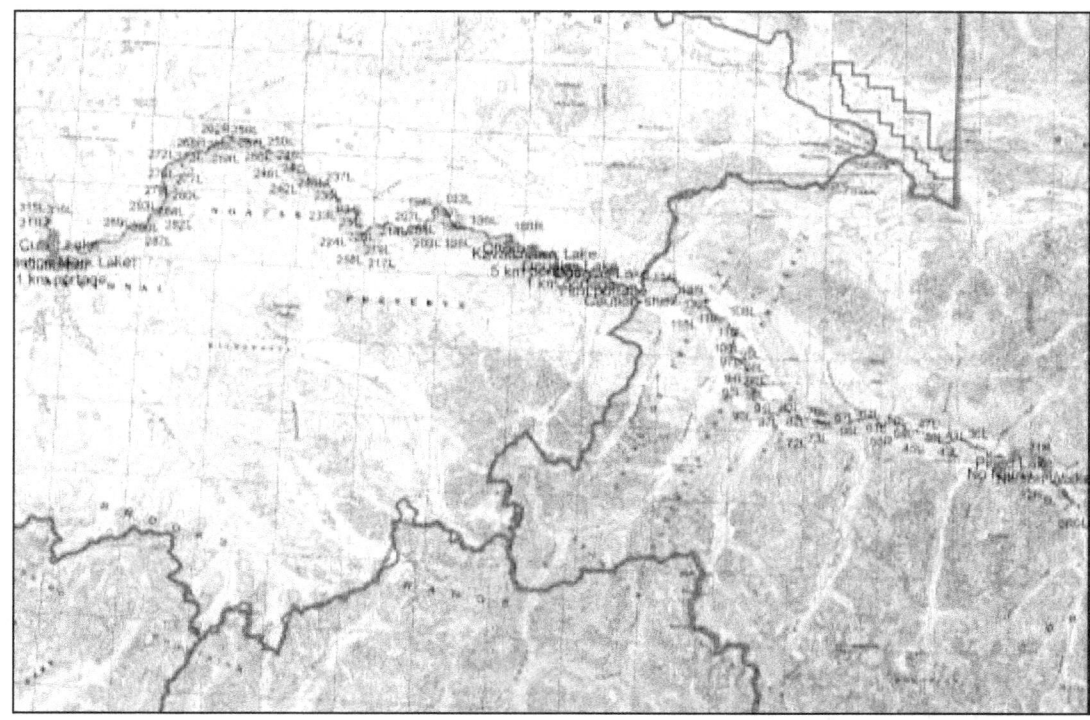

Figure 2. The Noatak River corridor route traveled on the by survey crews in June 2010. Surveys were conducted from east to west, moving down river.

Sampling Design

Bird survey methods were designed after North American Breeding Bird Survey (BBS) roadside survey routes (Sauer et al. 2008) adapted for river corridors and by methods developed by the Alaska Landbird Monitoring Survey (ALMS, Handel and Cady 2004), Guldager (2004) and Mitchell et al. (2009). Landbird monitoring will occur along riparian corridors to target the areas of greatest species diversity and abundance (Boreal Partners in Flight 1999). Landbird surveys used variable circular plot methods (Reynolds 1980) with limited inference space along riparian corridors as per Guldager (2004).

In addition, staff collected data on vegetation and environmental variable at bird survey points. The purpose was to classify bird habitat at survey points. Although no plans to use this data exist presently, this information will be archived and used in the future to improve our understanding of breeding bird-habitat relationships and the effects of invasive plants and climatic changes on bird populations. Environmental data will be used in bird population models to examine factors that affect bird detectability.

Finally, surveyors collected some information that will not be used by ARCN. Bird surveyors collected distance information for each bird detected. This will contribute to the ALMS program developed by USGS that uses distance sampling methods to estimate landbird species density across the state of Alaska (Handel and Cady 2004). ARCN does not use this method because recent analysis of bird survey data from Denali National Park and Preserve has demonstrated major violations of distance sampling assumptions (Hoekman and Lindberg 2011). Instead, ARCN will test the use of repeat surveys using multiple crews to re-sample the same points in the same season to generate landbird population estimates.

Survey points were spaced approximately ½ mile (0.8 km) apart to ensure that birds could not be easily detected at adjacent points and to limit autocorrelation between points. In addition, points were placed approximately 100m from the river bank and on both sides of the river to reduce disturbance from river noise. Surveys were conducted east to west while moving down river. Each survey point was repeated up to three times (once per crew) throughout the survey period and repeated surveys were conducted at least two days apart.

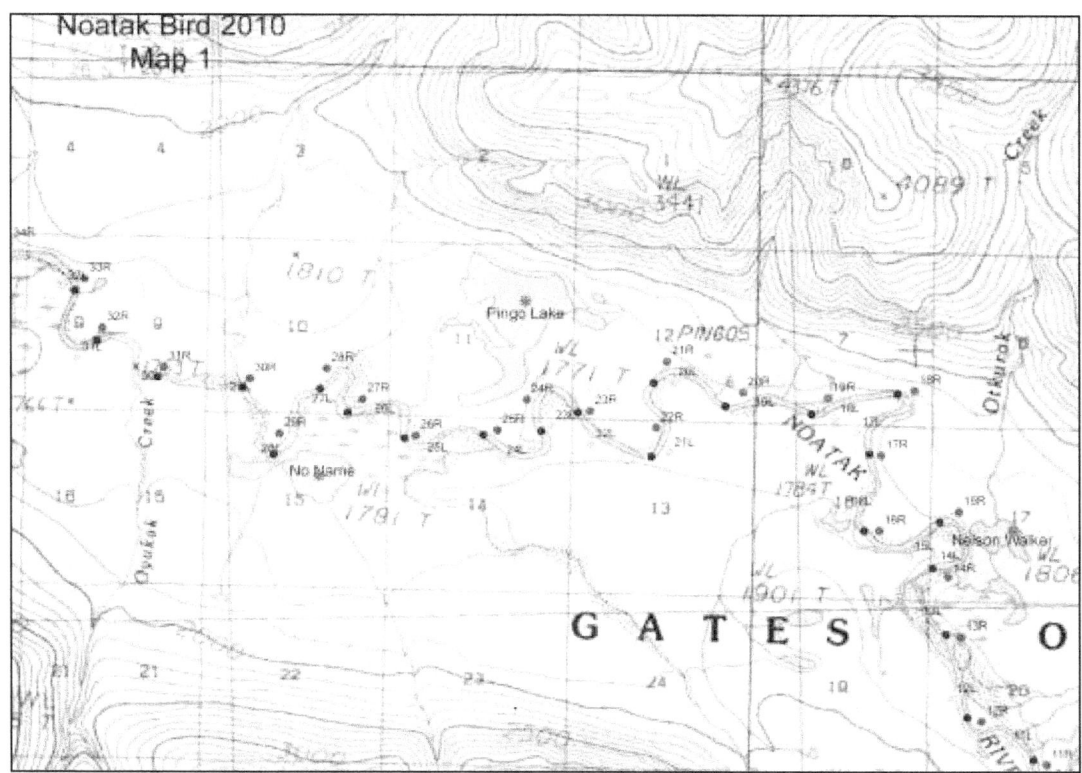

Figure 3. Example of potential survey points along the Noatak River, June 2010. The river flows right to left (east to west). Points on river-left are marked in green and river-right in red. Not all points were surveyed. Actual survey points were selected according to several critera (see text). Black points represent the river channel and were for navigational purposes.

Field Methods

In the field, six personnel were divided into three crews of two people. Both members of crew 1 conducted bird surveys. Crew 2 included one bird surveyor and one vegetation surveyor and crew 3 included one bird surveyor and one browse surveyor.

All crews were transported to Nelson Walker Lake (67.650529° N, -155.317168° W) in GAAR via floatplane on June 10, 2010 and floated the Noatak River to Cutler Lake (67.884696 N, -158.351270 W) in NOAT (Figure 2). Table 3 summarizes crews, routes and survey dates (see Results).

All crews travelled in inflatable canoes and carried gear and provisions for approximately 20 days. Crew 1 left Nelson Walker Lake on June 11. This crew was responsible for establishing survey routes. A survey route is defined as a set of points (approximately 8-12) that can be reasonably surveyed in a single day. This crew selected actual survey points from a suite of

5

"potential" survey points pre-established in a GIS and loaded as waypoints onto handheld GPS units (Figure 3). Actual survey points were selected in the field based on accessibility, safety and based on whether they met sampling design criteria (i.e., adjacent points were ½ mile distant and were 100m from the river's edge). Surveyor's attempted to select points on both sides of the river and alternated left and right sides, when possible.

Crew 2 left Nelson Walker Lake on June 13 and repeated surveys established by crew 1. Similarly, crew 3 left Nelson Walker Lake two days later (June 15) and repeated surveys established four days earlier by crew 1. Crew 1 communicated survey points/routes to following crews via satellite phone text message and by relaying points to the NPS ranger station staff in Bettles, AK. Crew 1 physically marked survey points with fluorescent colored pin flags. For ease of navigation, they used surveyor's-type flagging to mark nearby vegetation and river access points. All flagging was removed by crew 3 after surveys were completed. If crew 3 was unable to visit a particular point and, consequently, could not remove flagging, they relayed this information to ranger station staff in Bettles who later removed the flagging at their convenience.

Bird Surveys

Bird surveys were conducted by NPS staff and volunteers experienced with identifying birds by sight and sound (Figure 4). Bird surveyors will be referred to as "observers" throughout this report. Bird surveys were conducted between 2:00 and 9:30am. Upon arrival at a point, observers remained quiet for 1-2 minutes to allow disturbed birds to settle. Observers used laser rangefinders to establish a 100m radius around them prior to the point. Then, birders recorded all birds detected (aurally or visually) in a 400m radius during a 10min interval. For each individual bird detected, observers recorded the species, time of detection, type of detection, horizontal distance and compass bearing of each bird. Observers identified birds to species expect for redpolls and scaup because of the difficulty in distinguishing between Common (*Acanthis flammea*) and Hoary Redpolls (*A. hornemanni*) and Greater (*Aythya marila*) and Lesser Scaup (*A. affinis*), respectively. These species were lumped and recorded as either "redpoll species" and or "scaup species." Unidentified species were recorded as "unknown bird." Type of detection included singing, calling, visual, winnowing, drumming, flyover, aerial display aural and aerial display visual. To estimate bird distance, birders used laser rangefinders to either directly measure the horizontal distance of the bird from the observer or to estimate distance based on pre-measured landmarks within the survey area. In addition, birders qualitatively rated background noise (see Table 2), which may influence an observer's ability to hear birds.

Figure 4. An observer conducts a bird survey on the banks of the Noatak River in Gates of the Arctic National Park and Preserve. The survey point is marked with a pink pin flag.

Vegetation Surveys

Vegetation and browse surveys were completed while observers conducted 10min bird surveys. One member of crew 2 was responsible for classifying vegetation cover at two scales: within 20m radius and from 20-100m radius distant from the survey point. First, the vegetation surveyor used a range finder to identify landmarks within the 20m and 100m radius circles. Then, the surveyor classified all ground cover into six broad categories: water, bare ground, rock, snow/ice, litter and vegetation. Vegetation was further classified according to Viereck et al. (1992) Level III classification (Table 1, Figure 5). Ground and vegetation patches had to cover ≥ 5% of the area in each respective band to be included.

Within the 20-80m area and for each vegetation cover class identified, the vegetation surveyor listed the two dominant vegetation species in each of seven lifeforms. A lifeform is defined as tree, tall shrub, low shrub, dwarf shrub, sedge/grass, moss/lichen or bare ground. In addition, for all trees, shrubs and tree saplings the vegetation surveyor recorded the average height (in m) of each species. Within the 20m area, the surveyor identified and recorded any species that comprised ≥ 5% of the area, including each species average height, if applicable.

The vegetation surveyor recorded additional information on macro- and microtopography characteristics for the 100m radius area. For each macrotopography feature identified, the surveyor estimated the percent area included in the classification. Macrotopography classification included: summit or ridge, plateau (high flats), shoulder slope, upper slope, lower slope, toe slope, drainage, basin or depression, flat/fluvial, standing water, river or stream and human modified. If present, microtopography characteristics were noted. These included frost features (i.e., hummocks, frost scars and boils), ice and peat mounds (i.e., rocky outcrops, mounds caused by wildlife), drainage or erosion related features (i.e., water tracks, riverbed cobbles), polygons and water (i.e., islands). In addition, the vegetation surveyor noted any disturbance related to fire, flood, wind, landslide, animals, insects, disease or human and classified disturbance as "minor" or "severe." Finally, the vegetation surveyor measured the slope and aspect of the plot using a compass with inclinometer.

Browse surveys were conducted by a member of crew 3. The browse surveyor was responsible for assessing animal browsing pressure on shrubby vegetation. To do this, the browse surveyor selected up to 20 shrubby plants near the bird point and examined stems for signs of browse. For each plant examined, the browse surveyor recorded 1) distance from the point, 2) bearing from the point, 3) species, 4) height, 5) maturity class (whether or not 50% of anticipated annual growth was expected to be >3m above ground), 6) dead class (no dead, less dead than alive or more dead than alive) and 7) plant architecture (broomed, browsed or unbrowsed).

Table 1. Viereck et al. (1992) level III vegetation classification used to describe habitat at bird survey points on the Noatak River, June 2010

Class I	Class II	Class III	Description
Forest	Needleleaf	Closed needleleaf forest	Over 75% trees conifers; canopy 60-100%
		Open needleleaf forest	Over 75% trees conifers; canopy 25-59%
		Needleleaf woodland	Over 75% trees conifers; canopy 10-24%
	Broadleaf	Closed broadleaf forest	Over 75% trees broadleaf; canopy 60-100%
		Open broadleaf forest	Over 75% trees broadleaf; canopy 25-59%
		Broadleaf woodland	Over 75% trees broadleaf; canopy 10-24%
	Mixed	Closed mixed forest	25-75% trees conifers/broadleaf; canopy 60-100%
		Open mixed forest	25-75% trees conifers/broadleaf; canopy 25-59%
		Mixed woodland	25-75% trees conifers/broadleaf; canopy 10-24%
Scrub	Dwarf tree	Closed dwarf tree scrub	Minimum 10% cover dwarf trees; canopy 60-100%
		Open dwarf tree scrub	Minimum 10% cover dwarf trees; canopy 25-59%
		Dwarf tree scrub woodland	Minimum 10% cover dwarf trees; canopy 10-24%
	Tall	Closed tall scrub	Shrubs over 1.5m (5') tall; shrub canopy 75% or more
		Open tall scrub	Shrubs over 1.5m (5') tall; canopy 25-74%
	Low	Closed low scrub	Shrubs 20cm-1.5m tall; shrub canopy 75% or more
		Open low scrub	25-74% (or down to 2% if little/no other vegetation)
	Dwarf	Dryas dwarf scrub	Shrubs <20cm tall; *Dryas* species dominant dwarf shrub
		Ericaceous dwarf scrub	Ericaceous species dominant dwarf shrub
		Willow dwarf scrub	Willow species dominant dwarf shrub

Table 1 (cont'd). Viereck et al. (1992) level III vegetation classification used to describe habitat at bird survey points on the Noatak River, June 2010

Class I	Class II	Class III	Description
Herbaceous	Graminoid	Dry graminoid herbaceous	Grasslands of well-drained, dry sites, e.g., South-facing bluffs
		Mesic graminoid herbaceous	Moist sites, but usually no standing water; tussocks often
		Wet graminoid herbaceous	Wet sites; standing water; wet tundra, bogs, marshes, fens
	Forb	Dry forb herbaceous	Dry sites, usually rocky, well drained; mostly tundra
		Mesic forb herbaceous	Moist sites without standing water; mostly in forested areas
		Wet forb herbaceous	Wet sites, usually with standing water for part of the year
	Bryoid	Mosses	Vegetation cover dominated by mosses
		Lichens	Vegetation cover dominated by lichens
	Aquatic	Freshwater aquatic herb	Vegetation submerged or floating in fresh water
		Brackish water aquatic herb	Brackish water
		Marine aquatic herbaceous	Salt water

Figure 5. Common dominant Viereck et al. (1992) level III vegetation classification types (see Table 1) encountered at bird survey points along the Noatak River, June 2010. A) water, rock and bare ground on the river cutbank, B) open low scrub, C) Dryas dwarf scrub, and D) mesic graminoid herbaceous

Environmental and Other Data

All crews collected environmental data at each survey point. Each crew recorded cloud cover, precipitation, temperature, wind speed (NOAA), wind direction (Table 2) and, if present, collected Labrador tea (*Ledum spp.*) phenology data. Crews classified up to ten plants as vegetative, flowering, fruiting or dispersing seed.

While standing at the pin flag marking the point, each crew also recorded a GPS waypoint (NAD83, decimal degrees) and took photos. These waypoints documented "actual" survey locations, which may have differed from pre-established GPS locations. In addition, crews took one photo in each cardinal direction and one of the ground. Photos are a means of documenting landscape characteristics for the purposes of detecting change. These "baseline" photos may prove valuable in the future for examining changes in vegetation structure, such as shrub encroachment, fire impacts or other changes on the landscape. Consequently, this may help explain any changes in bird community assemblages detected over time.

Finally, while traveling between points, surveyors recorded notable wildlife, including all birds detected while on the river.

Table 2. Environmental variables recorded by observers at each bird survey point.

Attribute	Description	% Occurrence
Wind Speed	No wind	26
	Slight	31
	Wind felt on face, leaves rustle	28
	Leaves in constant motion	13
	Raises dust, small branches move	2
Wind Direction	East	49
	North	30
	South	12
	West	8
Sky Condition	Clear	28
	Scattered clouds	34
	Overcast	33
	Fog	5
Precipitation*	None	95
	Drizzle	4
	Light showers	1
Background Noise	None	7
	Barely reduces hearing	64
	Noticeable reduction of hearing	26
	Prohibitive (greatly reduced hearing)	4

*Precipitation data was not available for all points (see Results/Environmental Data)

Data Management

All data sheets were scanned and stored in electronic format. Bird data was proofed directly on paper data sheets and then entered into a Microsoft Access® database. The data was proofed a second time to reconcile data entry errors. The database was developed by an NPS database manager, who stored and safely backed-up the data. Database development, data proofing and data processes were completed in January 2011. Habitat and browse data booklets have also been scanned and stored but no efforts have been made to enter vegetation data (including phenology information and observations made between survey points). This work has been deferred.

All GPS units and cameras were downloaded and waypoints and photos stored appropriately. All photos were geotagged to their respective survey waypoint using the software program GPS-Photolink® v. 4.3.7 (GeoSpatial Experts Inc.). This program tags a photo with its geographic location by synchronizing the time between the camera and GPS to determine the latitude and longitude of each photo. We created three products with this software: For each photo taken we created 1) a watermarked photo stamped with relevant information about that photo (date, time, river name, latitude/longitude, crew number, route number, point number, etc.). In addition, for each route we created 2) a shapefile for use in a GIS and 3) a KMZ file for Google Earth®.

Data Analysis

Data presented in this report are not rigorously analyzed. A more thorough analysis of the data is intended after several years of data have been collected. However, we provide extensive summaries of the data to aid in planning future survey efforts in the Arctic Network.

We summarized environmental data simply. Categorical variables such as wind speed, wind direction, cloud cover, precipitation, and background noise are presented as the most frequently occurring conditions (mode). Temperature, the only continuous variable, is presented as a single mean (± SD) and daily ranges (minimum and maximum).

Prior to summarizing bird survey data, we censored all bird detections noted to have been observed at a previous survey point and all those of birds flying over the survey point. After censoring, all summaries included in text, tables and figures are presented as raw data. We examine basic relationships between variables but do not present a thorough analysis.

Vegetation survey data has not been entered or summarized. It will remain stored and available for use in the future.

Results

Survey Effort

Survey crews completed 444 separate bird surveys on 16 routes between 11 June and 29 June, 2010 (Table 3). Each route included 9 to 13 survey points, totaling 167 distinct points.

Table 3. Number and dates of bird surveys conducted by three crews on the Noatak River, June 2010

Route	# Points	Crew 1 Date	Crew 1 Points Completed	Crew 2 Date	Crew 2 Points Completed	Crew 3 Date	Crew 3 Points Completed
1	8	6/11	8	6/13	7	6/15	8
2	10	6/12	10	6/14	8	6/16	9
3	10	6/13	10	6/15	9	6/18	10
4	10	6/14	10	6/16	8	6/19	8
5	10	6/15	10	6/17	10	6/20	9
6	10	6/16	10	6/18	10	6/21	10
7	10	6/17	10	6/19	9	6/22	10
8	9	6/18	9	6/20	8	6/23	9
9	10	6/19	10	6/21	10	6/24	6
10	12	6/20	11	6/22	10	6/25	10
11	11	6/21	11	6/23	11	6/26	11
12	11	6/22	11	6/24	11	6/27	5
13	11	6/23	11	6/25	10	-	0
14	11	6/24	11	6/26	11	6/28	7
15	12	6/25	12	6/27	12	6/29	10
16	12	6/26	12	6/28	12	-	0
Total	167		166		156		122

Environmental Data

Environmental conditions during surveys were generally good (Table 2). Observers ranked wind speed along all available categories; however, for the vast majority of surveys (85%) wind were described as 'wind felt on face, leaves rustle' or calmer (<1 – 11 km/hour or a ranking of 1-3 on the Beaufort wind scale; NOAA). Wind direction was primarily from the east and north. Cloud cover conditions were mixed between clear skies, scattered clouds and overcast conditions. Fog was present during 5% of surveys. Precipitation data was not collected at every survey point because data sheets did not include a space to record precipitation conditions. However, precipitation information available for 426 surveys indicate that rain only occurred during 5% of surveys. Temperatures ranged from 28 to 70°F and averaged 47 ± 7°F (SD; Table 4). Background noise was present during almost all surveys. Observers rated background noise in the middle two categories ('barely reduces hearing' or 'noticeable reduction of hearing') for approximately 90% of surveys. Common sources of background noise included mosquitoes, water (i.e., creeks, river) and wind.

Table 4. Minimum and maximum temperatures (degrees F) recorded each day at bird survey points on the Noatak River, June 2010.

Date	Minimum	Maximum
June 11	52	70
June 12	43	60
June 13	38	60
June 14	38	54
June 15	40	59
June 16	34	56
June 17	41	61
June 18	28	59
June 19	37	56
June 20	30	56
June 21	31	62
June 22	32	62
June 23	34	62
June 24	37	62
June 25	40	68
June 26	32	59
June 27	31	52
June 28	37	60
June 29	31	54

Bird Surveys

Prior to summarizing bird survey data, we censored all bird detections noted to have been observed at a previous survey point (n = 10) and all those of birds flying over the survey point (6.9% of all detections). After censoring, observers amassed 7277 individual bird detections of 56 species. The appendix lists all bird species detected during bird surveys. The number of species and the number of individual birds detected by each observer both varied by as many as 30 species and 645 individuals, respectively (Table 5). Up to 17 species were detected on a single point (when summed between observers). Over 90% of all detections were aural detections of singing or calling birds. Three percent of detections were visual detections. Detections of winnowing birds and aerial displays made up 1% of detections. Twenty-seven percent of bird detections were made within the first minute of the 10-minute survey and 51% were made within the first three minutes (Figure 6). In the last three minutes, observers added an average of 2.5 bird detections per survey.

Table 5. Variation in survey effort and bird detections by observers conducting surveys on the Noatak River, June 2010

Observer	Points Surveyed	Species Detected*	Individual Birds Detected*
1	123	46	1598
2	165	76	2243
3	165	64	1783
4	157	58	1653

*includes detections of all unknown species, which are lumped into a single category

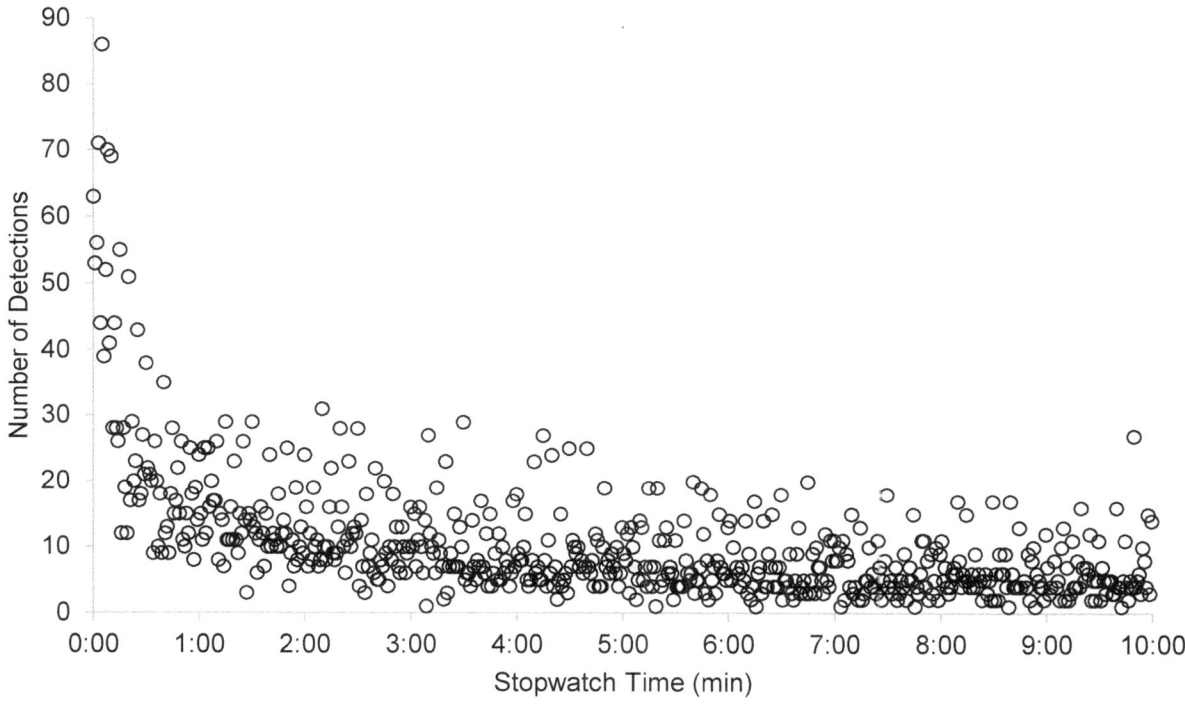

Figure 6. Bird detections during 10-minute surveys conducted on the Noatak River, June 2010. Each point represents the total number of bird detections made during a single second. Data is compiled for all observers and all surveys conducted June 11-29, 2010.

The total number of bird detections varied by date but not time of day (Figure 7). The total number of detections per survey point declined throughout the survey period by 0.5 bird detections per point per day (Figure 7B; linear regression: slope = -0.48, intercept = 15.84, R^2 = 0.83). Therefore, if observers completed 40 points per day (4 observers x 10 survey points), they were detecting approximately 20 fewer birds each day throughout the survey period. There was no significant linear trend in total bird observations throughout the survey day (Figure 7A).

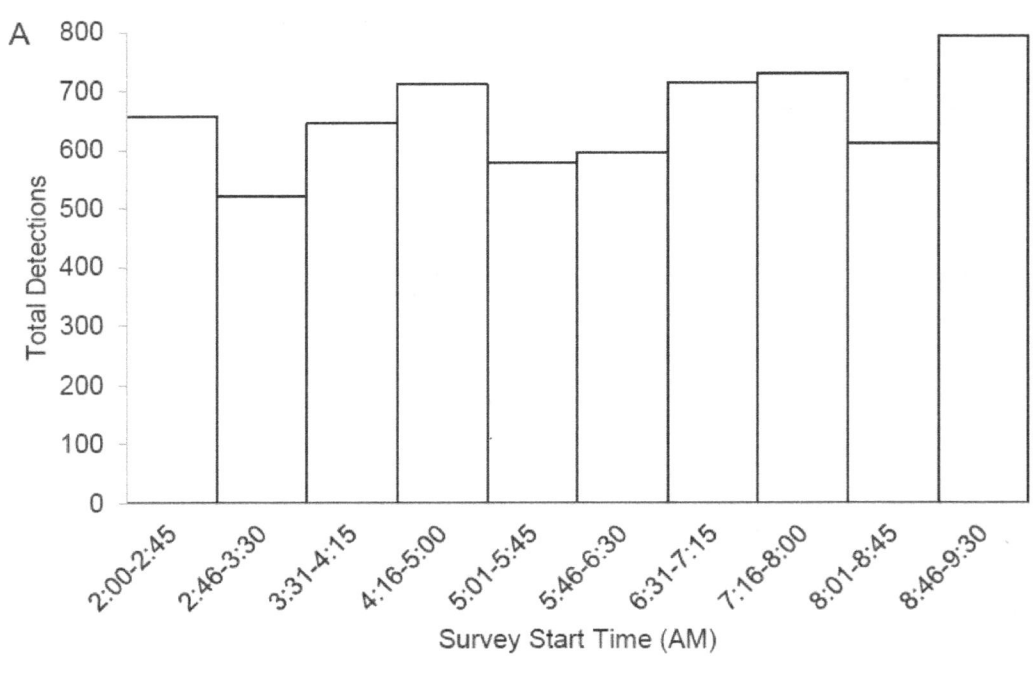

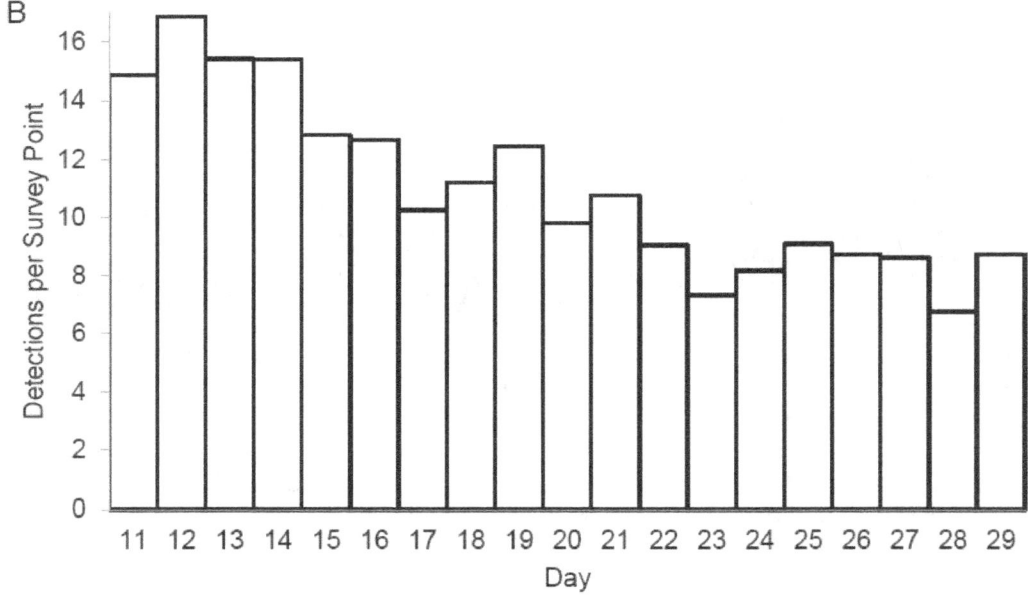

Figure 7. Total bird detections related to survey day (date) in June 2010 and survey start time during the same period on the Noatak River. To account for variation in the number of survey points completed each day on the y-axis in Figure B, we divided the total number of detections by the total number of survey points completed on that day.

Seven bird species had >200 detections (see Appendix). White-crowned Sparrows (*Zonotrichia leucophrys*) and American Tree Sparrows (*Spizella arborea*) were the most commonly detected species, with >1000 detections each. The next most-common species, Redpolls had 358 detections. Savannah Sparrow (*Passerculus sandwichensis*), Orange-crowned Warbler (*Oreothlypis celata*), Arctic Warbler (*Phylloscopus borealis*) and Gray-cheeked Thrush (*Catharus minimus*) also had >200 detections. The number of detections classified as "unknown" was high and totaled 469, the third most commonly detected "species." The total number of detections throughout the survey day appeared to differ for some common species (Figure 8). For example, American Tree Sparrow, Redpoll and Orange-crowned Warbler appear to be detected more often later in the survey day, whereas Gray-cheeked Thrush detections appear to decline in the middle of the survey day. However, a more formal analysis of these patterns is necessary to determine density estimates for these common species.

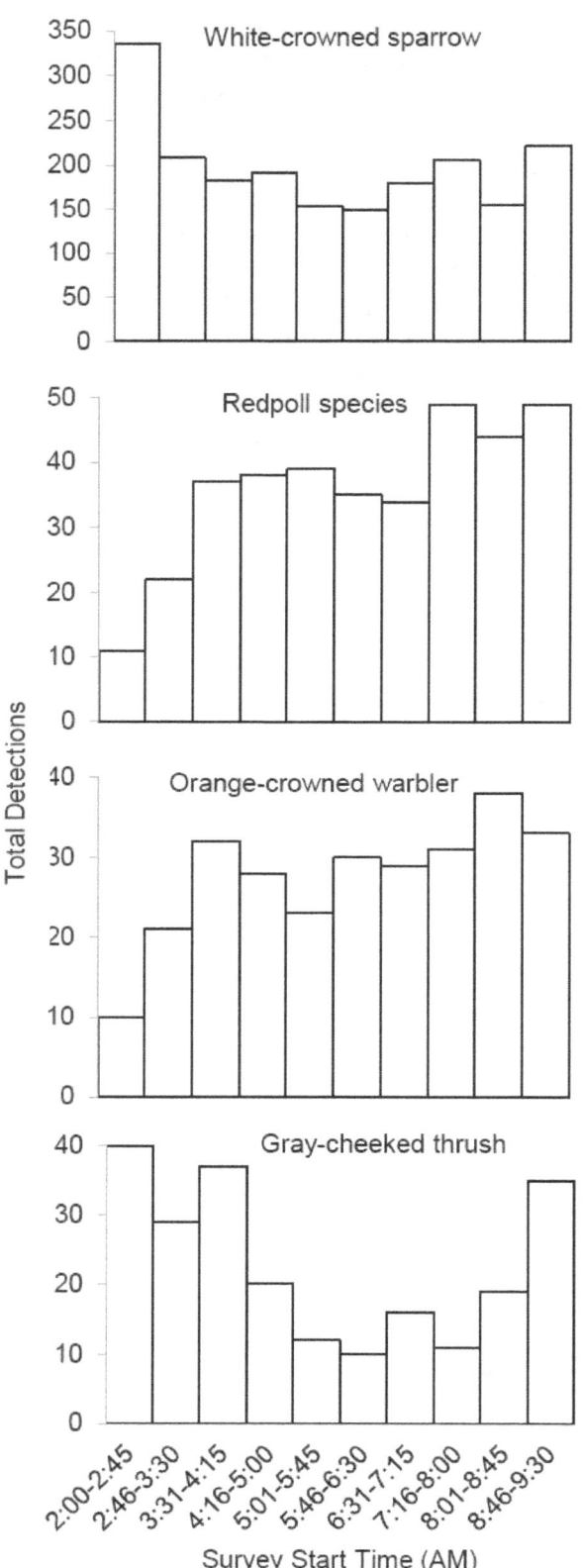

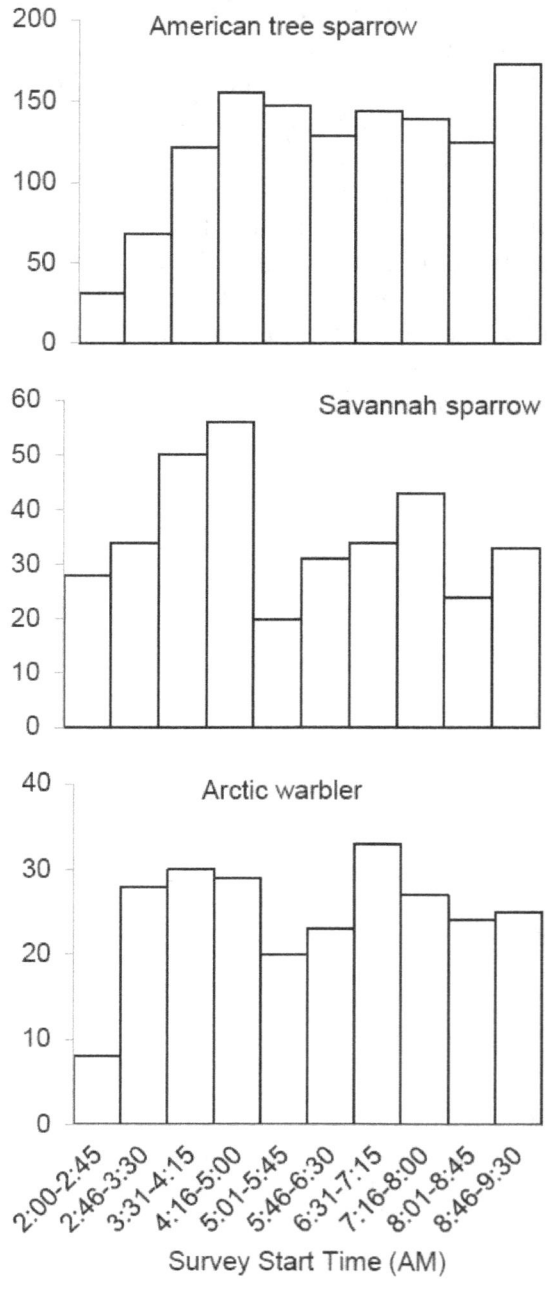

Figure 8. Total number of detections of the seven most commonly detected bird species on the Noatak River, June 2010, categorized by survey start time. Note differences in the scale on the y-axis for each species.

Discussion

Overall, the 2010 field season successfully met objectives. Our first objective was to complete one river corridor survey and establish survey points that will be used for long-term monitoring efforts. Three survey crews completed one river corridor survey along the Noatak River in GAAR and NOAT, completing 444 points on 16 survey routes. Locations of these survey points were marked with a GPS and stored for long-term use. Subsequent survey efforts on the Noatak River will use these points to replicate surveys.

Second, we tested survey methodology to determine the feasibility of repeat surveys along remote rivers for long-term landbird monitoring. We found that repeat river-based surveys are feasible and will likely yield sufficient data to meet overall project objectives. Once established, we anticipate sampling in subsequent years will require less logistical planning. However, the nature and cost of river-based surveys will likely effect year-to-year sampling efforts. Safety and river accessibility will be important factors during all surveys. Extensive training in bird identification, field methods and boating skills are required for all crew members prior to the field season. In addition, finding sufficient numbers of trained crew members with the necessary backcountry skills and availability to conduct the 2-3 week long surveys will be challenging. River conditions vary inter- and intra-annually and survey efforts will not be as reliable or consistent as road-based surveys, such as BBS. In addition, river-based survey efforts are costly and fluctuations in annual budgets may impact long-term survey efforts.

Survey efforts will continue in ARCN park units in FY2012. Additional river corridors that we are planning to sample include the Kobuk (Kobuk Valley National Park), Itkillik (GAAR), John (GAAR) and Nimiuktuk (NOAT) Rivers. However, consideration is being given to alternative field sampling methods that would allow the extent of our inference to expand outside of riparian habitats. For example, including hike-able transects through tundra or wetland would likely target a different suite of avian species and may allow us to model population trends for additional arctic species.

The long-term objectives of ARCN landbird monitoring vital sign includes 1) determine annual long-term trends in density and frequency of occurrence of 5-10 of the most commonly detected landbird species along selected river corridors across ARCN during the breeding season (June), 2) determine annual long-term trends in landbird species composition and distribution at selected sites across ARCN during the breeding season (June), and 3) improve our understanding of breeding bird-habitat relationships and the effects of invasive plants and climatic changes on bird populations. Bird survey data collected on the Noatak River will help us meet these objectives and will be valuable for long-term landbird monitoring in the arctic.

Literature Cited

Boreal Partners in Flight Working Group (BBS). 1999. Landbird Conservation Plan for Alaska Biogeographic Regions, version 1.0. http://alaska.usgs.gov/science/biology/bpif/conservation/index.php (accessed 6 September 2011)

Fancy, S. G. and J. R. Sauer. 2000. Recommended methods for inventory and monitoring of biological resources in national parks. National Park Service Inventory and Monitoring Program. Fort Collins, CO.

Guldager, N. 2004. Assess landbird diversity, density and habitat within Gates of the Arctic National Park and Preserve. Progress Report. National Park Service, 201 First Avenue, Fairbanks, AK.

Handel, C. M., and M. N. Cady. 2004. Alaska Landbird Monitoring Survey: protocol for setting up and conducting point count surveys. Sponsored by Boreal Partners in Flight. Unpubl. Protocol. USGS, Alaska Science Center, Anchorage, AK.

National Oceanic and Atmospheric Administration (NOAA). Beaufort Wind Scale website http://www.srh.noaa.gov/mfl/?n=beaufort (accessed 19 September 2011)

Mitchell, J. S., J. L. Allen, M. Flamme, N. Guldager. 2009. Firebird: Collocating and correlating fire, avian and mammalian long-term monitoring in the Arctic. Poster at the Fire Ecology and Management Congress, October 16, 2009.

Hoekman, S.T. and M.S. Lindberg. *In Press*. Point transect sampling for monitoring passerine birds in Denali National Park and Preserve: an assessment of 2002-2008 pilot data. Natural Resource Technical Report NPS/XXXX/NRTR—20XX/XXX. National Park Service, Fort Collins, CO.

Reynolds, R.T., J.M. Scott, and R.A. Nussbaum. 1980. A variable circular-plot method for estimating bird numbers. Condor 82:309-313.

Sauer, J. R., J. E. Hines, and J. Fallon. 2008. The North American Breeding Bird Survey, Results and Analysis 1966 - 2007. Version 5.15.2008. USGS Patuxent Wildlife Research Center, Laurel, MD.

Sillett, T. S., R.T. Holmes, & T.W. Sherry. 2000. Impacts of a global climate change on the population dynamics of a migratory songbird. Science 288: 2040-2042.

Viereck, L.A., C.T. Dyrness, A.R. Batten, and K.J. Wenzlick. 1992. The Alaska vegetation classification. General Technical Report PNW-GTR-286. Pacific Northwest Research Station, U.S. Forest Service, U.S. Departement of Agriculture, Portland, OR,

U.S. Congress. 1980. Alaska National Interest Lands Conservation Act, Public law
96-487-DEC. 2, 1980. 94 STAT. 2371. www.r7.fws.gov/asm/anilca/toc.html

Appendix

Appendix. Bird species detected during point-count surveys on the Noatak River, June 2010. Some species show a null value for Total Detections because these detections did not meet censor criteria for this summary (see Methods/Data Analysis). We include them here because they contribute to species richness.

Common Name	Scientific Name	Total Detections
Unknown species		469
Greater White-fronted Goose	*Anser albifrons*	1
Canada Goose	*Branta canadensis*	
Tundra Swan	*Cygnus columbianus*	
American Wigeon	*Anas americana*	9
Northern Shoveler	*Anas clypeata*	2
Northern Pintail	*Anas acuta*	
Greater Scaup	*Aythya marila*	4
Scaup spp.	*Aytha affinis* and *A. marila*	11
Surf Scoter	*Melanitta perspicillata*	2
White-winged Scoter	*Melanitta fusca*	
Long-tailed Duck	*Clangula hyemalis*	17
Red-breasted Merganser	*Mergus serrator*	3
Willow Ptarmigan	*Lagopus lagopus*	107
Red-throated Loon	*Gavia stellata*	1
Pacific Loon	*Gavia pacifica*	7
Osprey	*Pandion haliaetus*	2
Northern Harrier	*Circus cyaneus*	10
American Golden-Plover	*Pluvialis dominica*	48
Semipalmated Plover	*Charadrius semipalmatus*	1
Lesser Yellowlegs	*Tringa flavipes*	143
Spotted Sandpiper	*Actitis macularius*	11
Upland Sandpiper	*Bartramia longicauda*	108
Whimbrel	*Numenius phaeopus*	50
Least Sandpiper	*Calidris minutilla*	11
Semipalmated Sandpiper	*Calidris pusilla*	9
Wilson's Snipe	*Gallinago delicata*	157
Parasitic Jaeger	*Stercorarius parasiticus*	4
Long-tailed Jaeger	*Stercorarius longicaudus*	11
Mew Gull	*Larus canus*	16
Glaucous Gull	*Larus hyperboreus*	15
Arctic Tern	*Sterna paradisaea*	61
Short-eared Owl	*Asio flammeus*	1
Say's Phoebe	*Sayornis saya*	8
Northern Shrike	*Lanius excubitor*	2

Appendix (cont'd). Bird species detected during point-count surveys on the Noatak River, June 2010. Some species show a null value for Total Detections because these detections did not meet censor criteria for this summary (see Methods/Data Analysis). We include them here because they contribute to species richness.

Common Name	Scientific Name	Total Detections
Gray Jay	*Perisoreus canadensis*	1
Common Raven	*Corvus corax*	13
Horned Lark	*Eremophila alpestris*	1
Bank Swallow	*Riparia riparia*	50
Cliff Swallow	*Petrochelidon pyrrhonota*	14
Arctic Warbler	*Phylloscopus borealis*	247
Northern Wheatear	*Oenanthe oenanthe*	1
Eastern Yellow Wagtail	*Motacilla tschutschensis*	55
Gray-cheeked Thrush	*Catharus minimus*	229
American Robin	*Turdus migratorius*	119
Bohemian Waxwing	*Bombycilla garrulus*	2
Orange-crowned Warbler	*Oreothlypis celata*	275
Yellow Warbler	*Dendroica petechia*	19
Blackpoll Warbler	*Dendroica striata*	2
Wilson's Warbler	*Wilsonia pusilla*	15
American Tree Sparrow	*Spizella arborea*	1233
Savannah Sparrow	*Passerculus sandwichensis*	353
Fox Sparrow	*Passerella iliaca*	95
White-crowned Sparrow	*Zonotrichia leucophrys*	1981
Lapland Longspur	*Calcarius lapponicus*	106
Smith's Longspur	*Calcarius pictus*	92
Redpoll species	*Acanthis flammea* and *A. hornemanni*	358

www.ingramcontent.com/pod-product-compliance
Lightning Source LLC
Chambersburg PA
CBHW080935290526
45795CB00007BA/2767